PET OWNER'S GUIDE TO THE
BORDER TERRIER

Betty Judge

RINGPRESS

ABOUT THE AUTHOR

Betty Judge, a farmer's daughter, has been involved with animals all her life, and, as well as her lifelong passion for dogs, she has bred and exhibited horses, ponies and cattle.

Betty acquired her first Border Terrier in the early 1980s, and she now has one of the largest breed kennels in the UK, with numbers ranging from 50-100 at any one time. The Plushcourt kennel was founded on one dog and four bitches of various bloodlines, and all the dogs owned by her descend from these five dogs. A British Champion came from the first litter she bred, and many more British Champions have been bred or owned by her, as well as breeding a number of overseas Champions.

One of Betty's greatest achievements was winning the Terrier Group at a General Championship Show with a Border Terrier bitch, who went on to gain her World title at the World Show in Brussels before returning to England.

Betty has handled dogs professionally in the UK and overseas, and she is an international Championship judge of the breed.

Photography: Sheila Atter

Published by Ringpress Books Limited,
PO Box 8, Lydney, Gloucestershire,
GL15 4YN, United Kingdom.

First published 1999
©1999 Ringpress Books Limited. All rights reserved

ISBN 1 86054 014 7
Printed in Hong Kong through Printworks Int. Ltd.

CONTENTS

SHOWING YOUR BORDER TERRIER **49**

5

Show training; Show equipment;
Presentation; Entering a show; In
the ring; A guide to the Breed
Standard.

BREEDING **57**

6

Responsibilities; The stud dog; Mating; Pregnancy;
Whelping; After the whelping; Weaning the puppies;
Eclampsia.

HEALTH CARE **67**

7

Recognising illness; Hereditary diseases; Common
ailments (Anal glands; Arthritis; Burns
and scalds; Canker; Car-sickness;
Constipation; Diarrhoea; Dog fights;
Fits; Heatstroke; Lameness; Parasites;
Phantom pregnancy; Pyometra; Shock;
Skin problems; Stings).

1 *Introducing Border Terriers*

The Border Terrier is different. He does not have the manicured, sculptured look of the other terrier breeds. He can hide his loveable character and independent nature behind a dour expression. His distinguishing feature is his otter-shaped head which, combined with a moderately broad skull, dark eyes and a strong muzzle, makes him one of the most appealing of terriers.

Borders possess a harsh double coat – essential for a working dog and easily maintained. They are healthy, active and very affectionate and they respond to love and attention. Training should be started early – and Borders generally are easy to train. They get on well with children, other dogs and other animals. If you cannot offer a suitable, loving home, and give correct attention to feeding, exercising and understanding your Border Terrier, then think very carefully about owning one of this wonderful breed.

ORIGINS

Border Terriers did not become a breed in their own right until the middle of the 19th century, when they became distinct from the other terrier breeds in the Border region, the area where Northumberland in England and Roxburghshire in Scotland join. It is believed that the Border, Bedlington and Dandie Dinmont Terriers, who all originated from that region, are distantly related.

It is assumed that they evolved from the terriers bred by the travellers and the rogues who roamed the Northumberland Borders. Later, Border Terriers were owned and bred by farmers and shepherds. The area they came from was the Coquet Valley and Borders were, in the beginning of this century, also known as the

Coquetdale terrier. Occasionally Border Terriers bred today will show signs of their ancestry by having a soft, linty topknot, which both the Bedlington and Dandie Dinmont have, and which is a distinctive feature of those two breeds.

Eventually, towards the end of the 19th century, the name Border Terrier became established, possibly due to the fact that the dogs were linked to the Border Foxhounds by way of two families, the Robsons and the Dodds, whose names are associated with the Masterships and Huntsmen of the Border Foxhounds. The terriers who worked alongside the hounds, who hunted in the hill country, were Borders, of course. The Border Terrier was used either to bolt or, sometimes, to kill and draw the fox. In hill country, sheep would be the main livestock and it would be essential to the farmers to keep the population of foxes down to save stock being killed by them.

THE EARLY YEARS

Once the Border Terrier had developed into a breed in its own right, and the name Border Terrier had become established around 1880, the breed started to appear in the show ring. Soon after this some shows put in separate classes for the breed.

The first Border Terrier was registered at the Kennel Club in 1913, but as an 'Any Breed or Variety of British, Colonial or Foreign Dog not Classified'; he was a blue and tan dog named Moss Trooper. Border registrations continued to rise and an application for a separate breed register was made to the Kennel Club in 1914 but was rejected. Eventually the Kennel Club's official recognition came in 1920. The Border Terrier Club was formed in that same year – but many enthusiasts of the breed did not agree with it. They believed that Border Terriers would be ruined if they became show dogs and that they would lose their working characteristics. However, they did become members – but, being determined to keep the working tradition of the breed, had it written into the rules that no show should be supported unless it provided at least one class for Border Terriers holding a Working Certificate, and that every Hunt in the North should have a representative on the committee. It is not known if these rules were ever imposed, and they do not exist today.

The Breed Standard of those days does still have a bearing on the breed today, as the first words were: "The Border Terrier is essentially a working terrier and, being of necessity able to follow a horse, must combine great activity with gameness." Today the first line of the Breed Standard reads: "General Appearance – Essentially a Working Terrier." Challenge Certificates were first given to the Breed at the Carlisle Show in 1920.

The outbreak of the Second World War had a huge impact on dog breeders due to food being in short supply. Registrations up to then were about three hundred Border Terriers a year. During the war years, dog shows were cut back and travelling was limited, which led to registrations being lower. Many of the large commercial kennels containing other breeds of dogs had to be disbanded and, so valuable bloodlines were lost. Luckily, the majority of Border Terriers were in the hands of small breeders who kept the breed on an even keel during the difficult war years.

The Border Terrier is an ideal family companion.

THE BORDER TERRIER TODAY

The popularity of the Border Terrier today seems to know no bounds. There has been alarm voiced within the breed about this increasing interest, mainly because, when any breed becomes very popular, this seems to bring its downfall. Serious faults start to appear as novice owners breed for the wrong reasons and flood the market, selling puppies to unsuitable homes, which then find their way into the rescue organisations. Popularity within a breed can also introduce health problems, as those breeding only for profit do not select a sound breeding programme.

Popularity in a breed can sometimes be as a result of a dog being seen on television. When Ch. Brannigan of Brumberhill won Reserve Best in Show at Crufts in 1988 it was feared by some Border breeders that there would be an upsurge in requests for the Border Terrier; thankfully, I believe this was not the case. Border Terriers have become popular due to their own easy-to-live-with attitude to life and, as families' lives get more complicated in this present age, a Border Terrier answers their needs.

THE BORDER TERRIER CHARACTER

Border Terriers are essentially working terriers, bred to hunt, to chase and to kill. They will go to ground if allowed to, they will go 'deaf' occasionally and use their own natural instinct and brain when they need to. A Border could be described as being a big dog in a small dog's body. Borders are excellent house dogs. They bark when anyone knocks on the door, but are not aggressive with people. They usually give a big welcome to visitors and then quietly carry on with what they were doing. Borders are not 'yappy' dogs, unlike a lot of other terriers. They are a man's dog, a dog a man would be proud to be seen with, and they are a lady's dog, as they can be loving, gentle and loyal, and many also make lapdogs, belying their terrier instincts. They excel with children, being long-suffering and willing to play long hours with them, even allowing themselves to be dressed up and made to look silly, just to be part of the fun. This makes the Border an ideal first dog, especially for children.

They can be totally devoted to their family or owner; their only demand is not to be left alone for too long. Being, in their ancestry, a pack dog, they like the company of another dog, be it of their own breed or any compatible breed. That is why I think they fit so well into a family environment, as then they are still part of a pack.

A very intelligent and dignified breed, Borders do appear to train you rather than the other way round; sometimes I think they know what you are thinking and almost do what you require without being told. To reprimand your Border you will only need a raised voice as they are, as a rule, extremely sensitive and have been known to ignore their owner for several hours, or even days, after having received a scolding, until such time as they decide to forgive.

Borders will not show or admit to pain. Puppies being taken for their vaccinations will never make a fuss or squeal, unlike a lot of breeds. My vet always says "Well, it's a Border and a Border never makes a fuss." I think that is why they are so popular with vets. As a breed they are generally clean and do not usually take long to house-train. They are good travellers in cars and enjoy going with their owners on outings.

They do integrate well with

Lively and active, the Border enjoys exercise but does not demand it.

other animals and many happily go to live with cats, but occasionally you do hear of a Border who will chase and kill cats – the terrier instinct is very strong. I have many Border Terriers that I have bred who have gone to live in harmony with all types of other animals – rabbits, guinea pigs, rats, mice, birds, chickens, sheep, cattle and, of course, horses and ponies.

Borders will 'sing' at times due, I think, to having lived with Foxhounds, who are well known for their vocal attributes. Mine tend to sing a couple of times a day for about 30 seconds to a minute, then all is quiet. They tend not to do this if they are on their own, but I have several Borders that have gone to families who play musical instruments and the reports are that they like to help the music by singing along with them. Even very small puppies in the nest will sing.

Borders are a very playful breed and they seem to retain their youthfulness into old age. They are very trainable, many doing Obedience and many more doing mini-Agility. There are several Borders who have excelled at this and have reached top competitions.

PHYSICAL CHARACTERISTICS

Border Terriers are active and lively and, when over puppyhood, will be able to take a lot of exercise. At the same time they do not *demand* it, as a lot of breeds do, so if, on an odd occasion, you could not give as much exercise as normal, they would not hold it against you. Borders are known to be greedy dogs, and therefore many become obese quite easily, so food intake should be monitored quite early on in life.

Their coats should be kept clean but, being wire-coated dogs, this means they do not pick up too much dirt. Unlike a lot of terrier breeds they have slightly longer legs, which also means they do not pick up dirt on the stomach. The colours of the breed also mean that they do not show the dirt, unlike some white-coated breeds. Border Terriers are hand-stripped (plucked) to keep their coats tidy, which also means you do not get shedding around the home. This is done usually twice a year. If you are unable to do it yourself, there are professional groomers who will do it for you.

FINDING YOUR BORDER TERRIER

Having made your decision to

Bitches may have an independent streak in their character. This bitch is blue and tan.

The male is full of character and responds well to training. This dog is grizzle in colour.

have a Border Terrier, you must then try to find a reputable breeder. This can be done in many ways; one of the best is by contacting one of the Border Terrier Breed Clubs, which often have details of litters for sale bred by club members. You should visit the breeder before buying, so that the breeder has a chance to make sure that you are suitable to have one of the puppies, and so that you may view the mother and pups before making your final decision.

Another way of finding a Border Puppy is to visit a dog show with Border Terrier classes scheduled, as you can then chat to exhibitors and meet their dogs. It will also give you the opportunity to see the different types, sizes and colours. However, possibly the very best way to find your puppy is by personal recommendation from someone who has actually purchased a puppy from a breeder of Border Terriers.

MALE OR FEMALE
As a breeder of Border Terriers, I constantly get asked for bitch puppies for pets. Unfortunately there is some misunderstanding as

Watch the puppies play to get an idea of their personalities.

to the behaviour of dog Border Terriers. When I ask the potential purchaser why they require a female, the usual answer is that dogs wander and do not have such good temperaments. I can assure them that they are wrong. I have yet to have a male Border Terrier wander – quite the reverse; it is more likely a bitch will have an independent streak and wander. I have found dogs to be best when it comes to having a pet; they have more character, appear to be more trainable, and do not come into season every four, five or six months, or have false pregnancies. Males are always chosen for Obedience training and mini-Agility by experienced trainers. Bitches can be quieter and more 'laid back' in temperament. So I would advise, when deciding on your new Border Terrier puppy, not to discount a male.

Obviously the decision must also take into account your own circumstances, whether you have other dogs, children or elderly relatives, for example. Discuss your choice with the breeder you are getting your puppy from. You will have a wider choice of puppy if you decide to have a male, as it seems that there are more male puppies born than bitch puppies.

CHOOSING YOUR PUPPY

If you want your Border Terrier to be purely a pet and a companion, then all that is required is a nicely-bred, well-reared puppy. It is rare these days to get a request for a puppy that is only required to work; usually the dog is to be a companion and, maybe, to do a little work, for example ratting and rabbiting, and this, as I have found with my own, Borders do without a second thought. I did have one puppy who went to its new home to be joined by two young ferrets so that they would be a team to work together clearing rabbits, so it was essential for the Border to be able to differentiate between a rabbit popping out of the hole and its friend the ferret!

If you decide you want to show your Border, you would be well advised to buy from a winning kennel, as the breeder will have knowledge, experience and advice to give you about the puppy's potential and will have some idea of how the puppy will develop. A puppy with show potential should catch your eye by the way he carries himself; he should be balanced and not exaggerated in any way.

Colour is a personal choice but always remember the saying 'a good dog is never a bad colour'. The blue and tan colour has become more popular in recent years for the show ring, possibly because this colour of coat is very easy to keep tidy, enabling owners to keep showing the dogs even though they may not be in the best of coats. A small patch of white on the forechest is quite normal and, occasionally, puppies have white tips on their toes which usually disappear when they get older.

Being asked, as a breeder, for a show puppy is a rather difficult order to fill. At eight weeks a Border puppy can show promise of fulfilling that dream, but a lot can happen between eight weeks and six months when it could make its debut in the show ring. The most difficult thing to predict is the teeth change and, to be able to be shown, a Border must have the correct dentition. From eight weeks to six months a puppy can change so many times and can vary at the ages it does so. One can only hope that the puppy chosen at eight weeks will retain its early promise.

2 Caring For Your Puppy

When the day comes for collecting your puppy it is essential that everything has been properly prepared. You should have decided where he will sleep, eat and exercise and where he will be allowed to go in the home. Start as you mean to go on; it will make it easier for the puppy to adjust to his new life. All dogs need a routine and, if this can be established from day one, it will make the whole transition much better for everyone.

PREPARATIONS

Before you collect your puppy you must make sure that everywhere the puppy will be allowed to go has no hidden hazards. The garden should be well fenced, as you will be surprised how small a hole a puppy will squeeze through. Gates should have wire mesh attached to stop the puppy escaping. Put any dangerous garden equipment out of reach and, in the home,

electrical wires and telephone wires always seem to attract. Many times I have been 'cut off' by puppies chewing the plug off the wire to the telephone; I am now an expert at mending telephones! Remove anything of value you do not want chewed.

SLEEPING ARRANGEMENTS

The first thing to decide is where your puppy is going to sleep; this is very important, as it is where your puppy should feel most safe and secure. It should be in a place that suits both you and the dog. It should be dry and warm with no draughts. Most owners choose the kitchen or utility room as a puppy's first sleeping quarters, as they have tiled or washable floors to accommodate any mistakes a puppy makes. It is also possible to fence off a small area in one of these two rooms so that the puppy cannot get into too much mischief during the night, and it will also assist in house training. This pen can be made from either a child's playpen or wiremesh panels, as the floor can then be covered with newspaper and the puppy's bed placed in the pen.

If you have not enough room for a pen, then a very good alternative is a collapsible, folding dog cage; this can be used anywhere, as it is fully transportable. If you get one large enough, a small puppy bed can still be put inside, until the puppy gets older. Most puppies, when started off in this type of cage, will enjoy sleeping in it for the rest of their lives; it seems to become their own house within a house. I have two cages open and available in my home all the time and invariably my dogs use them – that is, when they are not sitting on the armchairs!

There are many dog beds and baskets on the market which are equally good, except the wicker type which, given time, will be destroyed by chewing and can be dangerous. Bean bags can also be a source of 'good fun' as, if your puppy is inclined to chew

The big day arrives when your puppy must leave his littermates and travel to his new home.

bedding, a hole in a bean bag can soon become a snowstorm and, I can assure you, the 'beans' can be very difficult to clear up. The best I have found is the very hard plastic, kidney-shaped dog bed; puppies will chew the edges but will not destroy the bed. It can be wiped clean and disinfected easily.

A soft pad, or fleecy fabric, can be placed inside for comfort, which can be easily washed in a normal household washing machine and tumble-dried if necessary. It is best to have two pieces of inner bedding so that you can always have a clean bed at the ready. When I wash my dog bedding in the washing machine, instead of using a fabric conditioner in the final rinse, I add some disinfectant in order to rid the bedding of any germs or smells that may have lingered even after washing.

COLLECTING YOUR PUPPY

You will have arranged the time of collection with the breeder. I prefer my eight-week-old puppies to be collected around mid-morning, as this usually means the puppy will arrive at his new home in the early afternoon. This gives the puppy the rest of the day to acclimatise himself to the new environment. It will give him time to eat, play and sleep and explore his new surroundings before being left when he is put to bed.

It is best for the journey if you have two people, one to comfort the puppy, the other to do the driving without distraction. If you have to collect your puppy on your own, use either a cat basket or cage, so that the puppy will not jump about in the car and cause an accident. The basket can be put on the passenger seat, as the puppy will be happier to see someone, rather than travel completely on his own. The seat belt can be put across the basket to anchor it. The best bedding for the journey home is newspaper and a towel, just in case the puppy is sick. For small puppies on journeys to the vet for vaccinations, I have just recently started to use puppy trainer pads, which are waterproof-backed, very absorbent and, of course, disposable. Depending on the length of your journey, a bottle of water and small water bowl would be useful.

PEDIGREE AND RECEIPT

The breeder of your pedigree Border Terrier should supply you with a signed copy of your puppy's pedigree; they may also have received the registration document from your national Kennel Club giving the registered number and pedigree name. Occasionally, registering puppies takes longer and this document may not be available, but the breeder will be able to post it on to you, signed on the transfer section, so you can transfer the puppy into your name. The breeder should also supply you with a sales receipt, stating the details of the dog, the price paid and any special arrangements, guarantees or declared faults with the puppy.

INSURANCE

Dog insurance will usually cover the puppy for death, veterinary fees and, very important, third party. More and more puppy purchasers are now insuring their dogs; for a small amount each month they can have peace of mind that, if things do go wrong or accidents happen, they will not have huge veterinary bills that they cannot pay. There are many policies on the market; I have found the best are those that give straightforward cover without paying extra for the 'frills' attached. Third party insurance is

Give your puppy a chance to explore his new home – and to meet all the members of his new family.

essential for the dog owner, as many owners are unaware that, if their dog caused an accident and damage was done, they could be liable. It may be worth noting that some household contents insurance schemes do cover pets for third party insurance only, but not all.

ARRIVING HOME

When you arrive home with your puppy, give him time to explore his new surroundings, particularly his sleeping area. The part of the garden you will want the puppy to use while he is being house - trained is also an important place for the puppy to become accustomed to in the first few hours after arriving home. If you have children, do not allow them to maul, or even fight over, the puppy; keep everything as quiet and calm as possible. Do not have all your friends, family and neighbours around to see the puppy straight away. He will need to settle with you before having lots of strangers visit, who may bring unintentional infections to the new, unprotected puppy.

You can give your puppy a feed soon after arriving home but do not worry too much if he does not eat. Everything is new and he will be confused about not having any of his littermates eating with him. It is normal that puppies in their new home suffer a loss of appetite but this should be short-lived. Your puppy at eight weeks old will need lots of sleep, so allow him as much as he wants. Do not allow your children to touch the puppy when he is asleep in his bed; this is his space and, when he is in it, he should be given peace and quiet.

THE FIRST 24 HOURS

Your new Border Terrier puppy may or may not complain loudly when he is first left alone. He will miss the warmth, comfort and company of his littermates. If your puppy is in the house you will have made sure he is warm, but sometimes a warm hot-water bottle will be of help, encouraging him to sleep in his bed; a soft cuddly toy of around the same size as the puppy can help, something to cuddle up to like his brothers and sisters. The ticking of an old clock wrapped in a blanket may also help.

The main thing is that, if your puppy cries, do not give in to him; once you have, crying at the top of his voice will be his way of summoning you. More often than not, a Border puppy will not make a squeak, sometimes to the disappointment of his new owners. I had, on one occasion, a family who rang me a few days after collecting their puppy and told me that, after putting their new puppy to bed, they went upstairs and listened for the crying new puppy. All night they stayed awake because, if the puppy had cried, they had decided they would go and get the puppy and take him to bed. The next day the family were exhausted, but the puppy was in fine form having made sure he had a good night's sleep! Anyway, if your puppy does cry, it will be short-lived and he will settle to his new routine.

FEEDING

When you collect your puppy, the breeder should give you a diet sheet giving the details of how the puppy has been fed. Most good breeders will supply you with food for the puppy for at least a few days. Do try to stick to that diet, as a puppy's stomach is still delicate, and changing the food straight away may cause an upset. The breeder should also supply the

Do not change your puppy's diet until he has had a chance to settle.

dates when the puppy was wormed and the type of wormer used. Details of any vaccinations the puppy may have had should also be supplied, with a veterinary certificate.

BOWLS

You should have at least two bowls for your dog, one for food and one for water. While the puppy is small the bowls should be shallow-sided so that he can reach his food and water without stretching too far. When the puppy gets older you will need to get bigger and deeper-sided bowls. I do not advise using plastic bowls as these are easily chewed and puppies are likely to eat the plastic which will not help their health.

I prefer the heavier stone bowls for both food and water; they are not so easy to tip over and, when used for food, do not move so easily when the puppy pushes into the edges to eat the last little bits. They also are too heavy for the puppy to carry about in his mouth and play with. The only disadvantage is, of course, that they can break. The next best bowls are the stainless steel type; these are more durable but some Border Terriers like to 'kill' this bowl and strong teeth can soon give these dishes a 'frilled' or 'patterned' edge.

COLLARS

When your puppy is collected at about eight weeks old he will still be very small, so I do not recommend putting a collar on at this stage. In any case, the puppy cannot be taken out into any public place until he has had his second vaccination, so it is not necessary to put the puppy on the lead straight away. All the puppy should do is exercise in his own garden. However, if you feel there is a need to put a collar on, I suggest you use a soft cat collar; it will not fit for long as the puppy's growth rate at this age is quite surprising. Do make sure the collar does not get caught up on anything, as this will frighten and panic the puppy.

TOYS

Borders are quite destructive with toys, especially with the squeaky type. As adults, they can remove the 'squeak' in one go, so unless you supervise this type of toy, it will not last long. Solid rubber balls are reasonably long-lived and most Borders like to fetch balls. For chewing I provide the deep-fried knuckle bones; they last a

Border Terrier puppies can be destructive with their toys.

long time, do not smell and, once the dog has taken the fatty bits off, do not make a mess. These bones are very good when puppies are changing their teeth, as they get rid of the baby teeth and encourage the new adult teeth to come through. Rawhide chews should be given with caution, as I have known dogs to get them stuck and choke on them. I allow mine only supervised access to these and only give large, hard-pressed ones because, as they wear them down to a small end, they can then can swallow the remaining end and choke to death. Soft knotted ropes are a favourite, especially if the puppy has a friend to play tug-of-war with, and the

All puppies need toys to chew on – particularly when they are teething.

makers claim that they also clean the dog's teeth. It is not a good idea to give an old slipper or shoe because you may discover one day that your puppy has chewed your best shoes as he did not know what was old and discarded, and what was best and still in use.

HOUSE TRAINING

It is the first and the most important training you start with your puppy, as soon as you arrive home with him. It is up to you whether your puppy will become house-trained quickly – it depends on your free time, patience and vigilance. Effective house training requires the puppy to keep to regular feed times and sleep times (including during the day). As a rule, puppies will need to relieve themselves when they wake up, during play and after meals. It pays to spend as much time as possible, particularly during the first two weeks, to establish a routine. Always take the puppy to the same 'toilet area' and encourage him to relieve himself with some words such as 'get busy' or 'be clean'. Stay with him and reward him with 'good boy' and a fuss. When he has finished he can go back into the house to play.

Do not chastise a puppy for doing his toilet in the wrong place; a puppy will always indicate when he wants to relieve himself. Watch for the signs – restlessness, whining for no reason, raising his tail, sniffing the ground and circling. If the puppy makes a mistake, then tell him a firm 'no' and take him – do not put him – outside. It is best to clean the area thoroughly afterwards to remove all smells so that he is not attracted to the same place again. It would be wise to remember that, in house training and general training, some puppies will be easier than others.

VACCINATIONS

While the breeder may have done some or all of the primary inoculations, this is not always the case. It is advisable, if the puppy has had no vaccinations, to take him within 48 hours of arriving home to be checked over by your vet and to start the inoculation programme. Vaccinations can start at eight weeks old but every vet has his own thoughts on when they should be done, so take his advice as he is going to be the person looking after your dog's health in the future.

The primary vaccinations cover distemper, hepatitis, leptospirosis, parvovirus and parainfluenza. These are given in two doses, either two or four weeks apart; your own vet will tell you when the second one is due, also when it will be safe to take the puppy out into a public place. Your dog will then need annual boosters, given approximately one year after the primary vaccinations. Occasionally, a puppy may be affected by vaccinations, being off-colour and quiet; this usually only lasts a day but, if it continues for any longer, take the puppy back to the vet.

You must keep your puppy at home until he is fully covered for all those diseases, away from infections and viruses he may pick up if he mixes with other dogs or is taken out in public. Parvovirus is perhaps the most dangerous; although not as widespread as it was years ago, it still keeps rearing its ugly head with serious consequences.

Rabies vaccinations are not required unless you are taking your dog abroad as, at the time of writing this, quarantine in Great Britain is still in place. However, this may change, but, until that happens, no one will know the consequences.

GROOMING

The Border Terrier coat, being hard and wiry, really needs a strong metal-toothed comb and a stiff-bristled brush, otherwise you will be unable to get down to the skin when you do your grooming. As a puppy the coat is soft, so a small medium-bristled brush will be sufficient to clean and to teach the puppy to be groomed. Nail-clippers are also a useful tool; because Border Terriers have thick pads, they tend not to wear the toenails down, even doing lots of road work, so you will need to attend to trimming nails regularly.

3 *Adult Maintenance*

The competition in the dog food market means you have a huge choice of food for your Border Terrier. New varieties of dog food seem to appear weekly, all purporting to be better than the ones before.

Many of the new foods are perfectly balanced and fully nutritional, so the pet owner today can feed the best food ever developed for dogs. Feeding your Border Terrier comes down to you, the owner, your dog's personal choice and, of course, the most suitable diet for the wellbeing of your dog. I will describe some of the options.

DRIED FOODS

Over the last twenty years there has been a large swing to feeding your dog with a complete diet of specially formulated dry food. Some consist of plain, straightforward diets, while others are more up-market premium foods. All these diets do not need anything adding to them, otherwise it will upset the balance of nutrition. They can be fed either soaked or dry but, whichever way, it is important to ensure that your dog always has a plentiful supply of clean, fresh drinking water. Dried foods are supplied in either small pellets or ball shapes, with various nutritional balances depending on the age and size of dog, and including vitamins and minerals, so no extras are required. This type of food is increasing in popularity as it is extremely easy to administer.

Under the heading of dry foods, I include the flake type of food, which covers the pasta variety of dog food as well. These have to be soaked; some include dried meaty chunks and gravy to encourage the dog to eat them. This type of food is still quite popular. The other dry food is the moistened variety, which is fed dry, so large amounts of drinking water should be available as it does seem to make the dogs very thirsty.

MEAT AND BISCUITS

This method is no longer fashionable, although I know a few Border Terrier breeders who still feed this way. The meat can be fed raw or cooked. Frozen raw mince of various types of meat can be purchased at pet shops. I find chicken and rabbit flavours are best cooked and I cook mine in the microwave which saves time. Many owners feed tripe, either raw or cooked. All this type of meat is traditionally mixed with terrier-sized wholemeal biscuit or brown bread. This type of feeding may need extra vitamins added, and it obviously needs more time, thought and effort than other methods.

If you decide to feed your adult Border Terrier in this way, it would be advisable to enquire about the type of biscuit and mixers to add to the meat. They all have different additives and different ingredients and some are better than others. I myself always use a good-quality wholemeal biscuit, which can be either fed dry or soaked.

CANNED AND FOIL-SEALED FOODS

Canned dog food has always been very popular, mainly I think due to its convenience. There is a huge choice of canned dog food on the market and now the foil-wrapped dog food is also becoming an alternative to canned dog foods. Most of these foods claim to be complete in themselves but it is more likely that this type of feeding should be mixed either with biscuit or the specially formulated mixer biscuit, but it is best to follow the manufacturers advice on quantities for the size and weight of the dog. I always feed a good-quality canned food, as this way I find my dogs do not get stomach upsets. Some of the cheaper canned foods can contain a lot of jelly or gravy and, therefore, in the long run, are more expensive.

AMOUNTS

Each Border Terrier is individual in its feeding habits, so always follow the manufacturer's advice about the quantities to be given. Border Terriers are renowned for being greedy and more often than not get more food than they require. If they are allowed tidbits from the table, then this should be

Make sure your Border is supervised if he has a bone.

taken into account when giving the dog his main meal. Even 'treat' biscuits should be taken into consideration as, once a Border Terrier is allowed to get too fat, he will be difficult to slim down and, of course, your dog will not be as healthy.

HAZARDS

Because Border Terriers are prone to greed, there have been occasions when this has been their downfall. Never feed large pieces of food, as they will swallow this whole and choke to death. I once fed a particular type of small treat biscuit to one of my Border Terriers who swallowed it whole and it got stuck in his throat. If I had not been present the dog would certainly have died.

Border Terriers will not only scavenge, they will also steal off the table if the opportunity arises. I know of one family who lost their beloved Border Terrier when she helped herself to a nice large piece of cheddar cheese from the dining table; it got stuck and she choked to death.

BONES

Never give a Border Terrier a bone unless you are absolutely certain it is safe. I allow only one type of bone, the deep-fried knuckle bones which can be purchased from pet shops. Do not buy the shank type because Borders tend to rub off their face-furnishings when attempting to get the marrow from the centre.

EXERCISE

You will need to build up a routine of daily exercise gradually, starting from when he is a puppy,

To begin with, restrict exercise to playing in the garden.

but remember your very young puppy will be susceptible to growth damage if over-exercised while physically immature. I allow my own small puppies to play outside, providing the weather is suitable, in a large fenced area (similar to a garden) and they have toys, tunnels and safe bones to keep them amused.

Do not train the puppy on the lead too early. Mine do not go on a lead until they are at least fourteen weeks old, and then only for a few minutes. Normally they are taken for their first short walk at around five months old; then, gradually, their walks are

increased. At this age they can go for short walks among strangers and traffic, as this will educate them to all the new experiences they will have to face up to in their adult life.

Plenty of freedom running in the garden, or in a large enclosed area, is very important to the young dog's developing muscles. When your Border Terrier is fully mature, he should have plenty of fresh air, freedom to run in the garden and a good walk at least once a day. All dogs will benefit from this brisk daily walk – it is invaluable for the dog's mental development as well as for the physical advantages.

HEALTH CHECKS
Always keep a regular check on your Border Terrier's general health and condition, because if problems are noticed early, they are much easier to treat. Prevention is better than cure. Your routine grooming is probably the best time to check that all is as it should be. Otherwise, an examination by you at least once a week should be carried out.

TEETH AND GUMS
Normally a Border Terrier will start to change his teeth at around

*Adult dogs will appreciate
a brisk, daily walk.*

on the teeth his breath will smell, the teeth will become discoloured and eventually the gums will be affected, leading to infection. My own dogs' teeth are kept clean by several methods – safe bones, the specially-designed chews and, if tartar still accumulates, I have a special tool to scrape the teeth. Your vet would be the best person to advise you if you are in doubt; they do clean dogs' teeth but, unfortunately, will use an anaesthetic to do so, which is best avoided. Nowadays it is possible to buy dog toothpaste and I know of many owners of Border Terriers who clean their dogs' teeth daily, with good results.

four to four-and-a-half months. It is advisable to check which puppy teeth are loose and which have fallen out, and to see how the new ones are coming on. Inspecting the mouth will have been made easier by your early training and handling. When the puppy is teething he will be reluctant for you to examine his teeth due to the soreness of the gums, so be gentle with him.

When your puppy has changed his teeth, you will still need to check his teeth and gums regularly. The teeth should be kept clean and free from tartar. If tartar builds up

EYES

Always keep a check on your dog's eyes to make sure there is no discharge. Most dogs collect a little dry crust, or 'sleep', in the eye corner and this can be easily wiped away daily. Border Terriers are prone to a slight weeping from the eye, particularly if there is irritation from the hair close to it. It is best to pluck this away, otherwise the hair under the eye will become stained. If the eye looks in any way infected or cloudy, veterinary advice is required as quickly as possible.

EARS

The condition of the ears should be checked when grooming. Borders tend to get ear trouble when the coat is long, due to the hair growing thickly around the ear, which prevents air circulating. If your dog is scratching, shaking his head and holding an ear slightly away from the head, this would indicate that your dog has got one of the many problems of the ear and you should get veterinary advice. There are very good ear cleaners on the market, which will help to clear excessive wax and keep the ears healthy. If your Border has ear trouble it would be advisable to pluck away the close hair to allow air into the ear, which will also help the healing process.

NAILS

Toenails should be checked regularly, which also includes dewclaws if they have not been removed from the newly-born pup. Dewclaws are on the inside of the front legs about one to two inches above the foot. I have never had a Border Terrier born with dewclaws on the hindlegs as some of the other breeds have. Dewclaw nails are not in a position to be worn down and will occasionally

Nails need to be trimmed on a regular basis.

grow in a circle, or grow so long that they can be a nuisance to both dog and owner, as they can scratch your hand or arms very badly when you play with your dog.

Borders do not tend to wear their nails down, so they do need to have their nails trimmed on a regular basis. If the nails are allowed to grow long, the quick inside the nail also grows longer. The quick is the pink line in white nails; it is not visible in black nails. If this happens it means that the dog's nails cannot be trimmed back properly and, eventually, the foot will become out of shape and look untidy.

If you decide to trim the nails yourself, get the nail-clippers designed for the job, which you can buy from good pet shops. Great care should be taken not to cut too far back because, if you cut into the quick, the nail will bleed profusely and this bleeding will take a long time to stop. It will also be painful for the dog, who will then associate nail-trimming with pain and be reluctant to have the nails trimmed next time. If you have your dog professionally groomed you can get the nails done at the same time. The alternative is to get your vet to do them for you. If you want to do them yourself, get an experienced person to show you how to trim the nails correctly.

THE BORDER COAT

The coat of the Border has a natural appearance when compared to a lot of the other terrier breeds, some of which are very heavily trimmed. Being harsh and dense, it is easy to keep clean; a stiff brush will remove any dry mud.

The coat consists of a harsh wiry top coat and a soft dense undercoat. The texture varies; some Borders have short, very harsh coats, others have a softer and longer length of top coat, and there are many types between the two extremes. Colour can often have some bearing on type of coat. Blue and tans, for some reason, usually have harsher and easier coats to manage, hence the increase in blue and tan Borders appearing in the show ring. However, other colours of Border can have equally easy coats to manage and, often, the coat type is inherited. Coats may not settle until the puppy is one year old. I have a bitch who was very fluffy as a baby puppy and now she has one of the best coats in my kennel, but it took two hand-strips before the adult coat appeared.

Pet Borders are best hand-stripped twice a year, in spring and autumn. Many Border owners are unable to strip their dogs and so pay a professional groomer to do it for them. Not all groomers can hand-strip, so it is best to find out if they can before leaving your dog with them. I have been told by pet owners that, having left their Border at the grooming parlour to be hand-stripped, their dog had been clipped. This is a disaster for the Border coat as it will then re-grow soft, fluffy and pale in colour, completely altering the appearance of the dog. Obviously it is best if you can learn to strip your own dog but, if

HAND-STRIPPING YOUR BORDER TERRIER

Ready for stripping.

Chalk makes the hair easier to grip.

Take off a few hairs at a time.

The hair comes out quite easily.

The undercoat is a different colour.

The finished result.

you cannot, have your Border hand-stripped by a person who is experienced with grooming the Border breed. It may be worth asking the breeder at the time you purchase your puppy if they would be prepared to help you.

HAND-STRIPPING

If you decide to hand-strip your own dog, it is important to get yourself organised with all the equipment you will need. Decide where you are going to do the job – outside in the garage or garden shed would be suitable, with a non-slip table to stand the dog on and a non-choke slip lead to tie the dog to either a hook or ring attached to the wall. Make sure the dog is comfortable and secure before starting. A small pair of round-ended scissors will be needed to trim around the feet, and the delicate parts you cannot pull the soft hair from. A block of chalk, or a pot of chalk powder, either for wiping on the dead coat or on your fingers will help immensely, as it gives a much better grip, enabling you to pull the hair with greater strength, making it quicker and easier for both the dog and you.

I always start stripping the dog's coat at the back of the neck; this section is perhaps the easiest and contains most loose hair, working down the back to the tail. If the dog has not been stripped before it is best to do the easy parts first, so that the dog gets used to the pulling routine.

Borders are hand-stripped from the eyes back. The fore-face is not plucked. If your dog has very profuse face-furnishing then a pair of thinning scissors can be used to trim and shape the hair. The most difficult part of stripping the dog is the rear end; the trouser hair on the hind legs is a sensitive part; patience is required as you may only be able to pluck a few hairs at a time.

Tails should be stripped gradually, giving shape as you pull; do not be tempted to cut the end of the tail, otherwise you will spoil the appearance of the dog and give a shaving-brush effect to the end of the tail. The underneath hair, or 'flag' of the tail, should also be stripped off.

The pair of round-ended scissors are used to trim the long hair around the feet, producing a neat appearance. They are also used for the long hair which grows on the male dog's sheath and the female dog's vulva to finish the picture.

BATHING

Border Terriers, having a harsh coat, do not require bathing very often. I recommend that they are always bathed after a full hand-strip; not only does it remove any chalk left in the undercoat, but it will soothe the skin, particularly if the dog's skin is of the very sensitive kind. Some Border's skin can go very red after stripping and these dogs may need bathing two or three times in a suitable dog shampoo. This will help calm the skin.

Do not be tempted to bath your Border Terrier before a show; many novice exhibitors have been. It will make the coat soft and fluffy, which is not what the Breed Standard calls for. If you have to bath your Border before a show, do so at least two weeks before the day; this will give the coat time to settle and the natural oils time to return.

Occasionally Border Terriers have to be bathed for the simple reason that they have rolled in something disgustingly smelly, as they do, and even after a bath they can still give off an awful stink. A friend once told me that tomato ketchup rubbed into the coat neutralises strong smells on dogs' coats; while never having tried this method, I presume one has to remove the tomato ketchup afterwards!

THE VETERAN BORDER TERRIER

Cherish your veteran Border Terrier who will have given the best years of his life to your enjoyment. Now is the time to repay this; even in the latter years there is much pleasure to be drawn from your old dog. Normally Border Terriers live to a good age; thirteen to sixteen years is typical and I have heard of many much older.

As your dog grows older his needs will change and you should be prepared to adapt. Good sense should help you decide the amount of exercise to give. At any time from ten years onwards the older dog should be allowed to go for shorter walks and at his pace. Each dog ages at their own particular rate, so discretion and discernment is required.

Diet is perhaps one of the important changes you will notice as your dog ages. He will no longer require as much food. Teeth may not be as good as they were, so the type of food given should be considered. I feed my old dogs twice a day, as this allows the digestive system not to be overloaded with one main meal. Nowadays dog food manufacturers produce a specially-designed food for the veteran dog, which I know many Border Terrier owners feed with good results.

The veteran Border Terrier should be always kept comfortable and warm; never allow the old dog to get cold and wet. Place his bed where the temperature is constant and free of draughts. He will sleep longer, and more soundly than when he was younger. Many Border Terriers go deaf in old age, so he will not hear you when you go to his bed. If you need to wake him do so

The veteran Border Terrier deserves special consideration.

gently, otherwise he will be startled and frightened, which is very unkind.

If you have other younger dogs in the household, make sure the old dog is not left out but, at the same time, do not let the young dogs either annoy or disturb the old dog when sleeping. Protect the old dog from any boisterous activities from the younger dog.

It is important to keep the old dog well groomed and trimmed – it will help his wellbeing and also ensure that, if there are any external health problems arising, they will quickly be noticed, which may avoid any suffering and pain, and also they will be attended to earlier.

Finally, when your Border is failing in health and losing his quality of life, please do not hesitate about making the eventual decision to put him to sleep, if this is what the vet recommends. It is the hardest decision to make but never let your dog suffer at the end; you owe it to him to have a dignified departure from the world. A dog, who will have done for you everything ever asked of him or her, deserves an honourable exit.

4 *Training*

Start training your puppy as soon as you get him. If he came from an experienced breeder he will be used to being picked up, to standing on a table and being handled correctly, to having his coat brushed, his ears checked and cleaned, his feet being handled and his nails trimmed. If you do this at an early age, puppies will accept it as normal. When they are still small any resistance to handling is easier to cope with, which is better than having a fight later when they are adult. If you have trained them from an early age, they really do start to enjoy their handling and grooming sessions and it would be silly to give up the good work the breeder started. This handling will become invaluable if, in future, you decide to show your dog.

LEARNING RIGHT FROM WRONG

The puppy must learn, from the tone of your voice, whether he is doing the right or the wrong thing. Use a soft, jolly and encouraging voice when things are going to your orders, but use a deep, growling and strong voice when he does wrong. I do not believe a Border Terrier *ever* needs to be hit for a misdemeanour; I have found a growly voice quite enough to stop them doing what they should not be doing. They will then respond by trying to do what you require of them. It is all a matter of getting on to their wavelength so you can understand them and, at the same time, they can understand you.

They are a breed willing to please you all of the time but occasionally they get it wrong. If you ever need to scold a Border Terrier really hard, it is best to get hold of one ear and firmly push the dog to the ground, your voice growling and saying a loud "No". The dog will not forget this lesson and "No" will become a very useful command throughout the dog's life. You must always be 'top dog' or 'pack leader', otherwise your dog will become a nuisance to you and to others.

If you intend your puppy to live only in the kitchen until he is house-trained, do not confuse him by sometimes letting him in to other parts of the house. Where the puppy is allowed to go within the house needs to be clear to the dog, otherwise he will start to disobey you straight away. Do not allow the puppy to sit on the armchairs if, at a later date, you do not intend to let him do this. It will only confuse the dog and make him more difficult to train in the long term. Always be firm, never angry, with the puppy if he does something new that you do not approve of. He will begin to understand your rules and, of course, build a trust and respect towards you, which is the foundation of the future pleasure both you and your dog will enjoy together over the years to come.

COMING WHEN CALLED

Start to teach your puppy his name as soon as you get him and use it on every occasion. The puppy will very quickly know his name and respond when you use it. It is best to connect his name initially to nice things such as being made a fuss of, or having a tidbit and, of course, at food times. Once that first step is completed, you can then add the command "Come", which is one of the most important commands you need. If established early, it will become second nature to him. If a puppy does not respond in the early lesson, I find that if I squat down to his level the puppy will then happily come to my hand. Most puppies will have been taught this lesson by the breeder, at meal times.

When your puppy is called and he comes to you, always praise him. It will establish a pattern, because, as he grows older, he will be a lot faster than you and be able to run away, making it difficult for you to catch him. Always take a tidbit with you in a crinkly paper bag so, if you have trouble getting your pup to come, repeat the command and rustle the bag; he will always come to you then – but always reward with a tidbit and always put your hand on the dog and praise him.

If the puppy or youngster does disobey you and will not come, growl at him to catch his attention. Once you have his attention, change your voice immediately to a soft and encouraging tone and call him again, and this should do the trick. When he has obeyed you, give him a tidbit and praise. If your dog really does disobey you, no matter how angry he may have made you, never, never, never scold the dog when you do get him back; he will associate the scolding with coming to you, and be put off even more from obeying the order to come.

Give lots of encouragement when you start lead training.

LEAD TRAINING

I find Border Terrier puppies take to walking on the lead very quickly. As a breed they follow at your heels anyway, so an attached lead usually does not create a problem. I recommend that about twelve weeks old is the time for a puppy to start to wear a collar; even at that age their little necks are very soft and delicate. They will soon grow out of the one that fits them, so it would be better to wait until about six months of age before you buy an expensive collar.

When you start training your puppy to walk on the lead, walk him in his own garden so that he will be sure he has nothing new to face and will happily walk along with you. Encourage him and praise him as he walks well, but do not allow him to rush on and pull. If he puts up a fight, keep calm and talk to him, then persuade him to walk a few steps, then praise again. It will not take long for him to learn. This will build trust between you so that when he goes out into the big wide world and meets things that he is unsure of, he will look to you for reassurance, which is the bond you have created in those early lessons in the garden.

SIT

Dogs should be taught to 'sit'

The command "Sit" can be reinforced by gently pushing the hindquarters into the Sit position.

STAND

If you are intending to show your Border Terrier, you will also have to teach him to stand. Border Terriers are traditionally shown free-standing, as opposed to being stacked, but you can do either to suit your particular dog.

To teach him to stand free you will have to spend time getting the dog to stand correctly for quite a reasonable length of time. This can be done by baiting your dog. This means the dog is taught to wait longer and longer for the tidbit to be given, until the dog understands the command "Stand". If the dog sits down, just move him and start again; eventually the dog should learn.

However, if you cannot get your

whether or not they are to be future show dogs. It is a useful exercise, as it teaches the puppy that you are in control. I find Borders will sit naturally just by voice. If, however, your puppy does not understand, repeat the command "Sit" and gently push the puppy's hindquarters down into the Sit position and then reward with a tidbit. The puppy will learn quickly and you will find, after only a short time, he will know the command.

If you plan to show your Border Terrier, he must learn to stand in show stance.

dog to do this, you can always teach him to be stacked, but even then the dog will need to understand the command "Stand". It is best to do little and often of this training, otherwise the dog will become bored and start to resist.

The Down is taught with the aid of a tidbit.

DOWN

The Down is the next command after Sit. Start with your puppy at the Sit position. Have a tidbit in your hand which you then hold on the floor in front of the puppy. When the puppy goes down for it give the command "Down" followed by the reward and praise. When this exercise is repeated several times the puppy will go down without you having to put your hand to the floor, but reward and praise every time until it is firmly established. If the puppy will not go down at the start of this training, a lead can be used to give a downward tug, or apply pressure on the forequarters.

STAY

When you train your puppy to stay it is best at first to have him on a lead so you are in control. "Stay" is one of the very important lessons any dog should learn. Make the puppy either sit,

The Stay exercise should be built up gradually.

or go down, with the lead extended from you to the puppy; walk away backwards (facing the puppy) and repeat the command "Stay". When you get as far as the end of the lead, stand still for a few seconds, then ask the puppy to come, and give praise. Gradually lengthen the distance you leave the puppy, always give praise when he does it right. If the puppy breaks the Stay, take him back to where you left him at Sit or Down and repeat the exercise, but do not go so far away from him before you call him. This exercise will take time and patience; little and often is best as the puppy will become bored with it. It may be helpful if you use a hand signal as well as the command "Stay", which will help the puppy understand.

NOISE

One of the questions I am asked, when prospective owners of Border Terriers come to find out more about the breed, is if they are a noisy or yappy breed. Thankfully they are not. Of course they will bark when there is anyone at the door or any disturbance, but they do not bark for the sake of it, which makes them more desirable in this day and age when noise pollution is very much a problem.

If you have trained your puppy to stay on his own at night you should have established that he is happy and content to do just that. Occasionally a dog will object to being left at night by howling or barking; at this point, if you want to remain 'boss', you must be firm and assert your authority and tell the dog in no uncertain terms that he must be quiet, otherwise complaints from the neighbours may follow.

Border Terriers, as mentioned earlier, have a habit of 'singing' which goes back to their early heritage when they lived along with hounds. I personally do not find it offensive but I am sure there are many people who would and do. A solo dog does not seem to do it but two will, and although they will only 'sing' for about 30 seconds at a time, they may do it several times a day. They will stop when ordered but you should be aware of this, especially if you have close neighbours.

TRAINING CLASSES

Obedience classes are excellent if you are experiencing difficulty with your puppy. These classes are usually run by experienced trainers who will be willing to help you iron out your problems. If you are doing well with your training, these classes can also be helpful in socialising your puppy and they can be great fun, as you will meet other dog owners with a common interest. The classes are usually held in the evening and there are several standards, starting with beginners, and going up the grades as the dog's training develops. Quite a few people just go to get the basic training, but others continue into higher standards of training, going on to compete in Obedience competitions.

Ringcraft classes are for those people who wish to show their dog. They are usually run by experienced show exhibitors. They also socialise the puppies, which prepares them for when they go to their first show, where they will see lots of different breeds, which may be frightening. The trainers will give a lot of helpful advice on how best to show your dogs. They will go through the motions of judging your puppy, so you and your puppy will know what to expect. They will also teach you ring etiquette and, of course, you will meet other people with other breeds but with a common interest.

MINI-AGILITY

Mini-Agility has become very popular in recent years and Border Terriers have shown a great liking for this form of competition. Quite a few Border Terrier puppies I have bred have gone to owners with the intention of training them to do this sport, several of them reaching a very high standard and qualifying for top competitions.

This sport is definitely for the fit and active owner. A high degree of trust and training is required if you wish to compete. Many

The Border Terrier will respond well to advanced training such as being taught to retrieve.

Remember training sessions should be fun, and lessons should be interspersed with play.

THERAPY DOGS

A great many Border Terriers are registered as Pets as Therapy, or 'Pat Dogs'; under this scheme dogs can visit patients in hospitals and residents in homes for the elderly. This brings comfort to those who can no longer keep a dog, or those who miss their own dogs while in hospital. It has proved to be a great success and, as the Border Terrier has such a kind and extrovert temperament, they are ideally suited to this 'work'.

THE GOOD CITIZEN SCHEME

The Kennel Club in Britain has introduced the Good Citizen scheme to encourage a responsible attitude towards owning a dog. Similar schemes are offered in many other countries. The idea is for the dog to be trained to do certain simple exercises aimed at producing a well-socialised, well-behaved dog who will be an asset to the community.

owners do it just for the fun of it, with no intention of going into a competition. It involves the dog going round various obstacles, which are usually hurdles, a tunnel, an 'A' frame, a seesaw, a walkway and weaving poles. Mini-Agility is for dogs of a smaller height than Agility for larger breeds with, obviously, lower and smaller obstacles.

LIVESTOCK

The Border Terrier, being a very adaptable dog, lives happily in both town and countryside. Many people are attracted to the breed because of its rustic appearance. There are many Border Terriers

A comprehensive programme of socialisation will ensure that your Border Terrier takes all situations in his stride.

that live in rural areas and should be taught to be steady with livestock, for example, sheep, cattle and horses. This type of training has to be done by walking close to these animals and teaching the puppy that they are not to be chased. Your early training should have established that you are in charge and so, when you meet this kind of livestock, you will be able to stop your puppy from worrying them. Always introduce the puppy, on a lead and early in the puppy's life, to this kind of temptation. Owners of town-living Border Terriers should always be aware of the livestock hazard when they go out into the countryside.

5 *Showing Your Border Terrier*

In their leisure time, many people begin showing their Border purely as a hobby. The best and kindest thing to do before you start is to get expert advice about whether your dog is of show quality. This can be done by either going back to the breeder of your dog, if they are exhibitors themselves, or by going to one of the Club shows and asking for an unbiased opinion from one of the senior officers of the Club. It is better to find out before you start that your adored pet Border Terrier is not of the standard required to show, rather than suffer embarrassment in the show ring.

SHOW TRAINING

Once you have made the decision to show your Border Terrier, the first thing you should do is to start his training. Obviously this is much easier when the puppy is still young, but even older dogs train very easily, especially if they have been well socialised and have had basic training.

Border Terriers are judged on the table, so it is important to get your Border to stand happily on a table and be calm and sensible when he is handled. A table with a non-slip surface is most important and then you can move the dog to the posed show stance position and have his mouth looked at, and head, body, feet and tail handled. This should be done daily until he is completely at ease. Once you have established this, you will only need to do this exercise occasionally.

When lead training your Border for the show ring, it is necessary to teach him to walk on a loose lead at your side, both left and right sided. It is normal to show your dog on the left side, but occasionally judges will ask for a manoeuvre which will mean he will have to walk on your right side. On no account must the dog be allowed to pull on the lead, as the judge will be unable to assess movement, and your chances of doing well will diminish.

When standing your Border in line, it is traditional to 'free' stand the dog; this can be done by 'baiting' the dog. This means the dog stands still, keeping his concentration on you because of the promise of a tidbit. Training will need practice, so that the dog will stand for longer and longer until he receives the treat. If you cannot get your dog to do this, it is quite acceptable to 'stack' your dog, which means you physically pose the dog into the show stance on the floor.

SHOW EQUIPMENT

You will need a light slip lead or show lead, a metal-toothed comb or a pin pad, which are useful for giving your dog a last-minute groom, and a ring clip to hold your number. If you decide to progress to Championship Show level you will need other equipment, such as either a wire cage or travelling crate in which to keep your dog safe or a chain to secure your dog to his bench, a blanket for your dog to rest on, water and a drinking bowl and, if the show is a long distance from home, food may be required.

PRESENTATION

You will need to prepare your

A lot of hard work goes into training a puppy for the show ring.

Border Terrier's coat which should be presented in a clean and tidy condition. Your dog should not be bathed just before a show, otherwise you will soften the coat and this will go against the merit of the dog, as the Breed Standard calls for a harsh coat. Ideally the Border Terrier should be fully hand-stripped eight to twelve weeks prior to his first show, which will give a new coat all over, looking its best. Ensure also that the dog is not too fat or too thin. The dog should be in fit condition. About a week before the show the dog should be tidied, taking off any stray hairs not required, trimming the hair around the feet, and cutting nails back, so that the dog looks his absolute best. Do not forget your appearance too. Always wear clean and tidy clothes. Do not 'overdress' as this will detract attention from the dog. Shoes should be flat and comfortable, as you will be on your feet for a considerable time if there are large entries at the show.

ENTERING A SHOW

You must get the show schedules in good time and ensure you fill in the form very accurately. Mistakes may mean you risk disqualification. One very important point is that your dog must be Kennel Club-registered in your name before you can show your dog. Many owners think that just because the dog has been registered by the breeder, he can be shown. This is not the case. Allow plenty of time to get to shows and arrive early so your dog settles into the hustle and bustle of the show well before your class. A dog that is acclimatised to the atmosphere will always show better.

IN THE RING

Most judges have their own system of conducting a class but, as a rule, you will be asked to line up as a class; maybe the judge will also ask you all to move together before inspecting the dogs individually and asking you to move your dog on his own. You should make it as easy as possible for the judge to examine your dog so all the points of your dog can be assessed. It is normal for a judge to start at the head, which will include looking at the dog's mouth to see if the dog has the correct scissor bite. The judge will feel the body, forequarters and hindquarters. The feet, pads and the tail will also be examined. The

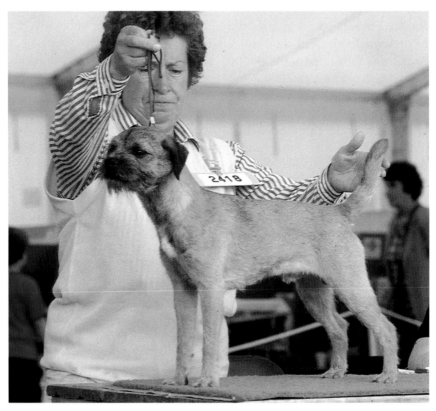

The judge will examine each exhibit in turn.

judge, with both hands, will span
the dog behind the shoulders and
lift the dog to assess his weight.

The judge will then ask you to
move the dog straight up and
down, or maybe in a triangle, in
order to see the dog's movement
from the front and rear and in
profile. When the judge has
reached a decision, the dogs will
be placed in order of merit. If you
do not win, be graceful in defeat,

congratulate the winner and
remember, next time you may be
the winner. If it happens to be you
that wins, enjoy the day. Judges'
opinions on dogs can differ widely
so, at another show with a
different judge, a completely
different result may be given. Your
Border, first and foremost, is your
friend and companion and,
whatever the judge's opinion of
your dog is, nothing changes that.

A GUIDE TO THE BREED STANDARD

Anyone who owns a pedigree animal is interested in the Standard against which their pet should be compared. If you have a show animal then this becomes even more important. This is a guide to the Breed Standard of the Border Terrier.

Dedicated breeders have closely guarded Border Terriers, in order to maintain exactly the first line of the Breed Standard regarding appearance. Borders should look like working terriers and be capable of doing the job they were bred for.

They had to be capable of following a horse, although the horses the Border Terrier was bred to follow would have been a slow, more substantial type of horse, not a thoroughbred; their gait has to have the soundness to enable them to do this with ease. They also need the proper temperament for this activity, so they are lively, spirited and of sound movement. I would add that they are easy-

The Breed Standard calls for a game, active dog with the appearance of a working terrier.

A classic otter-shaped head is typical of the breed.

going and amenable with humans and other dogs. They are also sound in mind, not excitable, not hot-headed, kind in disposition, calm in present-day situations.

The part of the Breed Standard which refers to the head is perhaps one of its most important statements. A Border who does not possess the classic otter head will lack type and could be just another terrier. It is the one thing that symbolises the breed. The skull is broad with a short strong muzzle, and a black nose is preferable, although a liver or a flesh-coloured one is allowed.

The eyes are dark, not prominent, not round, not too close together, but not too wide apart and have a keen but not a hard expression. The ears are not round, heavy and thick, but small 'V'-shaped ears which lie close to the cheek. They are not too high or close together (which would give a Fox Terrier expression) and not breaking the line of the skull. Ears should not stick out sideways or 'fly' as sometimes described.

As mentioned earlier, the mouth should have a scissor bite, with the upper teeth closely overlapping the lower ones and set square to the jaw. An undershot jaw means that the front teeth (incisors) of the lower jaw project beyond the front teeth of the upper jaw when the mouth is closed. Overshot means the front teeth (incisors) of the upper jaw overlap and do not touch the front teeth of the lower jaw, leaving a gap when the mouth is closed. A show Border should not have either of these faults.

The neck should not be so short that the dog appears not to have a neck at all, nor too long, giving an exaggerated swan-like appearance. The neck should be well set on, merging gradually with strong withers, forming a pleasing transition into the topline. The neck should not have an upper, arched portion of the neck, i.e. a crest.

The teeth are large and strong and should meet in a scissor bite.

The forelegs should be straight, not wide apart but not too close together either, and have moderate, clean, flat bone.

Borders have a deep body, but not too deep, so the breastbone is below the elbow. It is narrow and fairly long with the ribs carried well back but not oversprung. Long in rib, not short giving a barrel rib, nor a slab-sided or flat rib. The underline is gradual, not cut up like a whippet. The body is spanable, meaning that the dog can be spanned by both hands directly behind the shoulders, and not too large in rib, thus enabling the dog to be able to go to ground, and return to the surface after completing his work. The

loins, the part of the body between the last ribs and hindquarters, are strong,

The hindquarters give an impression of speed without loss of substance. They are long from hip to hock, short from hock to foot, and have a good bend of stifle without exaggeration. The feet are small and tight, not open, spread or flat, and have thick pads capable of standing up to a day's work.

The tail is probably best described as carrot-like in shape and is never docked. The coat is the dense, harsh, thick coat of a working terrier and Borders are coloured either red, wheaten, grizzle and tan or blue and tan. The size of dogs ideally ranges from 5.9kg to 7.1kg (13lbs to 15.5lbs) and bitches from 5.1kg to 6.4kg (11.5lbs to 14lbs).

6 *Breeding*

There is a theory that every bitch should have at least one litter in her lifetime. I have doubts about this because when you breed from a bitch you put her at risk – which, of course, includes the one litter you may think would be good for her.

RESPONSIBILITIES

Much thought should be put into deciding whether or not to breed a Border Terrier litter and it would be wise to get expert advice. Remember that you bought the puppy bitch as a pet. Was she sold to you by the breeder as a pet because she had a fault, or faults, that she might perpetuate in her puppies? If so, it would probably be unwise to breed from her, as no one should breed from inferior bitches.

Have you got the time and facilities to give to the bitch and puppies? Will you be able to find suitable homes for your puppies when they are ready to leave at eight weeks old? Will you have room to keep them after eight weeks if you have been unable to find homes for them? Will you also have the time and room to take puppies back if the homes you sold them to prove unsuitable?

Have you got the finances that you may need for veterinary care if things go wrong? You could end up having to have a Caesarean operation to deliver some, or all, of the litter. Should all the puppies die, you will have no puppies to sell to offset the costs of the operation and after-care, so you will be seriously out of pocket. Vets still have to be paid even if things go wrong, and veterinary care these days is very expensive. The worst thing that could happen is for your bitch to die, and quite a few bitches have when whelping, which could leave you to rear any orphan puppies that remain.

Do not be encouraged to breed from your bitch by people who say they would like a puppy from the litter, unless you are certain they mean it. So many times I have been told this and so often the people back out of having a puppy after the litter is born, leaving you with a litter which you had for their benefit.

Many people breed from their Border Terrier bitch because they would like to keep a puppy for themselves which, I think, is the best reason for having a litter.

I have, of course, detailed some of the disadvantages of breeding from your Border, but would like to add that giving birth is a natural process and the majority of bitches sail through whelping and very much enjoy having puppies.

If you are unsure about where to get expert advice, become a member of one of the Border Terrier clubs, whose secretary will be able to give you information and be able to guide you and put you in touch with someone in your area who will be able to help you.

It is best, I have found, not to breed from your Border Terrier until at least the third time she comes in season, at approximately eighteen months old, and ideally

Great care must be taken when assessing breeding stock.

before she is three years old. I often get asked by novice owners if they can use a stud dog of mine, only to discover the bitch is five or six years old and has never had a litter. It is madness even to think of starting at that age; apart from the fact that she would be unlikely to conceive, you would put a huge risk on the bitch's life. The slower-maturing breeds of dogs are quite often not bred from until they are five or six years old with no ill effects, but smaller breeds like the Border Terrier need to be bred from much earlier.

THE STUD DOG

Once you have got as much information as possible, you must set about finding the right stud dog for your bitch. If your bitch came from a reputable breeder, go back to them and ask their advice about what stud dog to use. It is always best to use a proven, experienced stud dog. Do not be tempted to use the dog down the road because he is close; he may be totally unsuitable. If you are going to breed a litter, try to do the best for your bitch. It will cost you more, in the long run, to breed a poor litter than it will to breed a good litter.

Go and see the dog before you need to mate your bitch and remember to take the bitch and her pedigree to the owner of the stud dog so that they can approve of her. Not all owners will allow their stud dogs to be used by all and sundry. Ask what the stud fee is and what conditions will be included; for example, do you get at least two matings if necessary and also, if she fails to have puppies, does the stud fee cover a free return. Most stud dog owners offer this, but not all. After you have made a decision about the stud dog for your bitch, inform the owner of the expected time your bitch will be in season.

When your bitch comes in season and before mating her, work out the time she will possibly whelp; also consider when you will be needing to start to wean the puppies (occasionally as early as two weeks) up to the time they may possibly go to their new homes.

There is a lot of time and work with puppies, so make sure you are going to be able to give it when they are born. It is not sensible to be away on holiday, or working, when you have a litter of puppies unless you have adequate help to look after them properly.

MATING

You must be vigilant so that you know when your bitch comes in season. Border Terrier bitches often have been in season for several days before the owners have realised it. They have subsequently taken them to be mated too late, which is disappointing if all the plans have been made.

You must check your bitch virtually every day for the start of her season. The first sign is the vulva swelling; some Border bitches' vulvas swell and do not show any signs of red discharge, others will show very little red discharge. Count from the day her vulva becomes swollen, just in case she is a bitch that has clear seasons. The bitch showing colour should be taken to be mated when the discharge becomes paler. I recommend to owners, if they find it difficult to monitor their bitch's colour, to use either a white tissue to dab the vulva morning and night to determine the colour change, or to put a white cover on her bed so that you can monitor the colour change. If your bitch shows no red discharge then you will really have to go by the days; ten to twelve days after coming in season is probably the best guide.

However, I have known several bitches who have been ready to mate and have been mated as early as six days into season and produced puppies from this one mating, but this does not happen very often.

Some maiden bitches, particularly pet bitches who have become very humanised, can be reluctant to be mated even though they are in full season and can be difficult. This is why it is best to use an experienced stud dog who will not be put off by the bitch trying to ward off his every advance. At the other end of the scale, there are maiden bitches that will throw themselves at the dog, which makes it much better for everyone concerned. This flirty kind of bitch must be watched all the time while she is in season as she will slip the net and find herself her own mate if given the chance, and I doubt if it will be your choice of dog!

Once the bitch has been mated, you must keep her away from the temptation of any other male dogs until she is completely out of season. In fact, it is probably wise to keep her away from any male dog all the time she is in season. I once had a visiting bitch to mate to one of my Border stud dogs, who subsequently whelped five puppies seven days early. They were predominantly brown like the bitch but had large white patches where they should not have been, and it was concluded that she had already mated herself to the next door neighbour's white and tan short-legged terrier, prior to being mated to her owner's choice of Border stud dog.

Mating dogs can alarm the very novice person, as not everyone is aware that, while mating, they 'tie' or 'lock' together, on average usually for about twenty to thirty minutes. I have heard of dogs being locked together for hours, although this is very rare. It is usual to have your bitch mated twice, approximately forty-eight hours apart; once this is done, take your bitch home and keep her secure and quiet.

Occasionally a bitch will, after being mated, have a red discharge from her vulva, even as late as three to four weeks after mating. Do not be alarmed, it usually indicates that the bitch is in whelp and there is activity within the womb. In the early days of pregnancy nothing should be changed, so treat her normally.

PREGNANCY

The gestation period of a bitch is sixty-three days or nine weeks, but you should be prepared for her to whelp anything up to five days early or four days late. My bitches, on average, whelp two days early.

Your bitch can indicate from as early as three weeks and as late as seven weeks that she is in whelp, so do not give up hope. Early signs are her teats becoming pink or purple, she could go off her food, there may be slight vomiting or she may become very quiet. On the other hand, she may show no signs at all and still could be pregnant. If she shows signs of being in whelp early, it could indicate she is having a large litter. On average you should, by six weeks, know whether she is in whelp or not.

Once you have determined that your bitch is in whelp, her feeding will need to be adjusted from approximately five weeks onwards. As the puppies grow bigger, she will not be able to take the amount she needs in just one feed. It is advisable to split her food into two meals a day, and even up to four feeds a day towards the end of her pregnancy. It is important to keep the bitch eating, otherwise she will not have the resources to draw on to give birth. In the final two weeks, exercise should be supervised so she is not overtired. Sensible exercise is good for her but taking her out and about, particularly in the car, is best avoided.

Depending on what time of year your bitch is due to whelp, her coat should be well groomed. If it is in the winter months and she has a full coat, it is advisable to strip her at about six weeks in whelp, as she may have to have a heated lamp over her and the puppies. If she has a full coat, she will find it too hot to lie with the pups and will sit out of the whelping box, which is not good for the pups. At this time the hair around her vulva should be removed to keep everything as clean as possible, ready for the delivery of the puppies. Towards the end of the pregnancy, your bitch will probably have a sticky clear discharge from her vulva; this is normal. Any other colour is not and may mean she could be aborting her puppies so a vet should be consulted.

WHELPING

As the expected date of arrival of your litter draws closer, you must try to establish where you would

Border Terriers generally take motherhood in their stride.

like your bitch to give birth, somewhere she will be settled and free from intrusion. Most bitches like to have a paw held and be supervised, but there are others who resent any presence or help; you will not know how your bitch will react until the moment comes.

At two days old, these puppies will divide their time between eating and sleeping.

It would be sensible to inform your veterinary team that your bitch is due to whelp, then, if you do need to consult them in the middle of the night, they are aware of the situation and are obviously better prepared to give help if required,

When the first stages commence there is nothing to do except sit quietly near your bitch and give her comfort and reassurance as and when she demands it. The first stages can last as long as twenty-four hours, when she will pant and tremble and dig up her bedding and look totally distressed. Do not be alarmed by this as it is quite normal. The next stage will be when the contractions start in earnest; with time they will increase and she will start to push. The first pushes will be light and then eventually get stronger, and a water bag may appear and then break, which will produce a clear liquid. Soon after this the contractions will get stronger, the time between them will be shorter and, eventually, what will look like a black bubble will appear, which will be a puppy.

If the bitch does not attend to it, and some will not, you must open the membrane covering the head and clean the mucus from

The puppies' nails must be trimmed so that they do not scratch their mother when they are feeding.

the puppy's nose. The placenta, or afterbirth, will be attached to the puppy by the umbilical cord. Most bitches bite the umbilical cord themselves and eat the afterbirth. If yours does not, after a few minutes it would be best if you cut the cord with sterilised scissors about an inch away from the puppy. Sometimes the afterbirth is not expelled with the puppy, but it should come before the next puppy. I always count the afterbirths as, if one is retained, it may cause problems and you need to tell your vet. Bitches eat the afterbirths which contain useful nutrients and help to get the bitch's bodily functions going again after whelping.

Do not allow your bitch to

strain strongly with no result for longer than one hour; a puppy could be misplaced or stuck. You must call the vet. I do not recommend that the novice breeder should try to do any internal investigations as you may cause serious damage. This is best left to your vet, who may be able to manipulate the puppy out if it is stuck or misplaced.

When your bitch has finished giving birth she will be exhausted and will want to sleep, if only for a short time. Providing she is happy for you to touch the puppies, it is up to you to see that all the puppies suckle. This is *very* important, for they receive the colostrum which contains antibodies from the mother and will protect them until they are old enough to be vaccinated. Do not forget to get the bitch out of the nest and allow her to relieve herself soon after whelping. I do not offer anything but clean water to drink when the bitch is giving birth, as a great many bitches actually vomit while whelping.

It may be wise for your vet to see the bitch and puppies soon after whelping; your vet will probably give the bitch an injection to ensure that any pieces of retained placenta are expelled.

Get the puppies examined for any abnormalities.

AFTER THE WHELPING
The newly-whelped bitch and puppies need comfort, warmth, peace and quiet. Do not keep interfering with the puppies as this can upset the bitch. She will need to be allowed to relieve herself at regular intervals. Some bitches will not want to leave their puppies even to do this, so you must make her, but keep her away from them for as little time as possible. As time goes on she will become more confident and will be happy to leave them for a short time.

Feeding the newly-whelped bitch can occasionally be a trial. After eating the rich afterbirths she may refuse food for a while and may go off her food altogether. At this stage I will try anything just to get her eating again. This can range from best fillet steak to a dry digestive biscuit. Normally, when they start to eat, they continue. If the bitch has had a large litter, she may not have had room to eat too much towards the end and these bitches will often eat the moment they have finished whelping. The bitch should be fed best-quality food in small amounts, as much as she will take; what you give now will assist in making a good supply of milk for the growing puppies.

WEANING THE PUPPIES

Any time after two weeks of age, and definitely by three weeks, you should start weaning the puppies. One of the most important things at this time is worming. If the puppies are carrying worms they will not thrive, and worming can be done as early as two weeks with a liquid wormer from the vet. They should be wormed at least twice more before they are eight weeks old.

When you start to feed the puppies you can offer them some warm puppy milk and, once they accept that, you should offer it twice a day to get them started, gradually increasing the number of feeds to four times a day. The other feeds should be warmed meat and I find the canned puppy meat ideal for this. Eventually I start to feed the complete puppy food which is a fine kibble, soaked with warm water at first, then gradually, as the puppies' teeth are through and strong, it can be fed dry for a change of texture. They must have clean fresh water at all times as it makes them very thirsty. The puppies should be fully

These three-week-old puppies have started eating solid food.

The littermates will learn social skills from playing together.

weaned and independent by eight weeks when they will be ready to go to their new homes.

ECLAMPSIA (MILK FEVER)

I have included this information in the breeding section of the book as it is only relevant to the breeding bitch. Borders are prone to this problem, though mostly only in a mild form; however, the bitch will still need veterinary attention.

This is a terrifying condition for the owner and can be fatal for the bitch. The blood calcium level of the bitch becomes too low, due to the puppies' demands for her milk and she begins to show nervous symptoms. To start with she may just look a little odd by twitching and shivering; she will be restless and may pant. This rapidly progresses to obvious staggering, a wide-eyed frightened expression and convulsions. It is essential that the vet is contacted immediately as an injection of calcium, usually directly into the vein, is essential to save the life of the bitch. She will respond very quickly and will be walking normally within a few minutes. However, once the blood calcium has been this low, the puppies should be weaned if possible, to ensure the eclampsia does not recur. Take the advice of your vet.

7 Health Care

One thing you must do, either just before, or very soon after, getting your Border puppy or dog, is to register with a suitably located, good vet. If you have no idea where to start looking, recommendations from other dog owners may help you. Make sure you have to hand details of the vet's telephone numbers, both for surgery hours and emergencies. Well-reared and carefully-bred Border Terriers are, as a rule, extremely healthy dogs, so hopefully your visits to your vet will only be annually for the necessary booster vaccination, worming and, perhaps, parasite remedies.

Your first appointment with your vet will be for your puppy's health check and primary vaccination. The vet will go over the puppy very thoroughly to check that he is in good health and that the first vaccination can be given. Most vets are excellent at handling baby puppies and will try to make the visit as stress-free as possible. If you feel the vet you have chosen is, for any reason, not satisfactory, then do not hesitate to change to another vet at the practice or to another practice. A dog owner should have full confidence at all times in the vet they use for their dog's health and wellbeing.

RECOGNISING ILLNESS

Hopefully, your puppy will be a healthy, happy dog and understanding his wellbeing will help you recognise when there is something seriously wrong with him. Occasionally dogs will just become under the weather, maybe will refuse a meal; do not offer anything else as this may make things worse. A dog who is off-colour is best given no food for twenty-four hours. After this time offer food again and you will find, in the majority of cases, the dog will be back to normal. It is essential that clean, fresh drinking water is available at all times; never leave a sick dog without water, otherwise he will dehydrate, creating more problems. If your dog starts to drink huge amounts of water for no sensible reason, vomits and there is blood present, or has continual serious diarrhoea, then you should consult your vet.

HEREDITARY DISEASES

Luckily, at present, the Border Terrier is not known to be afflicted by any of the common inherited diseases. However, as with any breed of dog, isolated cases of hereditary diseases have been reported. These include heart murmurs, hip dysplasia, Legg-Perthes disease, patella luxation, epilepsy and cataracts. There have also been cases of Progressive Retinal Atrophy reported from America. It seems that these reported problems are not a serious threat to the overall health of the Border Terrier, but responsible breeders are monitoring any incidence of them and, obviously, taking them into consideration in their future breeding plans.

Another occasional abnormality which is said to be hereditary is tails with kinks or bends in them. Puppies are usually born with them; some will improve and others get worse. As a pet it will have no consequence, but if you wish to show your Border it will disadvantage the dog.

COMMON AILMENTS

ANAL GLANDS

The anal glands are located on either side of the anus. Their original use was for scent marking and they still give off a distinctive smell, for instance when the dog is frightened. As a rule these glands are emptied by defecation but, if the dog's motions are soft and too loose, there is not the pressure on the glands which is needed to clear them. The symptoms are that the dog will have an unpleasant smell, he will drag his rear end along the floor, or will attempt to chew or lick near his tail area in order to relieve the irritation caused by overfilled anal glands. An abscess may occur if they are not cleaned. If you are unable to empty them yourself, it would be advisable to get your vet to do it for the dog's comfort.

ARTHRITIS

This is a complaint that usually

affects older dogs. A veteran Border will endure stiffness, but do not allow the dog to suffer unnecessarily as there are several remedies, purporting to be beneficial for this complaint, which are certainly worth trying.

BURNS AND SCALDS

The treatment for burns and scalds is the same as for humans. Rinse the affected area under a cold tap or hosepipe in order to take the heat out; if necessary, cut away as much hair as possible. In minor cases apply a suitable soothing ointment; in serious cases your vet must be consulted. A badly burned dog will be suffering from shock and should be kept warm and quiet in his bed or box.

CANKER

Border Terriers' ears should be checked regularly for problems. The word canker, over the years, has been used to cover any ear problems. As there are several different reasons for ear disease, the term canker seems outdated. If your Border is scratching, rubbing an ear, shaking his head, or has an ear held slightly away from the head, it would indicate an ear problem. Any of these symptoms could be caused by ear mites, a

fungal infection, or a secondary infection through scratching. There is a vast array of ear ointments on the market, some designed to treat specific infections better than others. For this reason veterinary advice is required. It is important to continue the full course of treatment to clear the problem.

CAR-SICKNESS

Border Terriers are normally good car travellers but small puppies can be car-sick, although I have had many that have never ever been

Border Terriers are generally good travellers, particularly if they are accustomed to it at an early age.

second primary vaccination and has full immunity, you will find the puppy learns to travel well. It is best done early in the dog's life; some dogs who have not travelled until later in life take a long time to adjust to the car and, in some cases, never ever travel well. Car-sickness tablets can be bought but, as a rule, they tend to make the dog drowsy, so they are not advisable if you are attending a show. I have used, with very successful results, herbal tablets for car-sickness. Do not feed your dog prior to travelling if he does not like the car as, for certain, he will be extremely sick and very distressed. The dog should be allowed time to relieve himself before travelling.

sick while travelling. Ideally your puppy should be taken for short distances in the car, either on another person's lap which is covered with a towel or blanket, or in a travelling cage or box. The puppy must be secure, not only for the dog's benefit but for road safety. Each time you take the dog in the car the journey should end with something enjoyable so that the dog associates the car with pleasure.

If you do this as soon as the puppy is allowed out after the

CONSTIPATION

If this happens frequently it probably indicates incorrect feeding, so your type of food and method of feeding should be questioned. Gnawing bones can seriously upset some dogs and, if this is the cause, then they should not be given. Change of exercise patterns can sometimes activate this problem, as dogs are creatures of habit and, if they have to wait too long to pass a motion, this can cause constipation. When a dog is constipated, occasionally it will pass a smearing of blood with the motion. As long as it is only a trace it will resolve itself but, if there is any considerable amount, then it should be considered serious.

Home remedies for an odd incident of constipation would be a teaspoonful of liquid paraffin or, for younger dogs, the laxative used for fur-ball in cats is very good. If the constipation persists, or frequently occurs, it would be advisable to consult your vet, as he may be able to suggest a new feeding regime which will alleviate the problem. It may be worth noting that I have heard of quite a few Borders who have been able to swallow rubber balls, parts of toys, and even stones, which caused constipation problems – and no amount of laxative will remove these objects!

DIARRHOEA

There can be many reasons for this condition. The dog's diet, or a change of diet, or eating something unsuitable can start a bout of diarrhoea which can be resolved by making the dog fast for twenty-four hours, giving glucose and water to drink so that he does not become dehydrated.

Start feeding again with light, easy-to-digest foods such as chicken or fish. Diarrhoea can also be a sign of serious problems such as gastroenteritis, parvovirus, worm infestation, foreign bodies in the gut and internal organ problems. Stress can also trigger diarrhoea, just as it does in humans. If your dog suffers from a persistent diarrhoea problem then veterinary help must be sought as, if it is left to continue for any length of time, the dog will dehydrate and become extremely ill.

DOG FIGHTS

The priority here is to separate the dogs without further injury to either people or dogs. Never shout when dogs are fighting – it only adds to the frenzy – or try to pull them apart. Borders, when fighting, are inclined to 'lock on' and, if they both have locked, this is the time to part them. You will need two people. If the dogs have collars, put a small stick under the collar and twist it. This will tighten the collar which will restrict the air flow to the neck and, once the dog cannot breathe, he will let go. If the dogs are in the garden a hosepipe can be used, initially to spray water on to the head and eyes. If this fails, spray the water onto the nostrils; once a dog cannot breathe he will let go. A bucket of water can do the trick, or dropping both dogs into a tank of water. Once separated, keep the dogs well away from each other and inspect the damage done.

Control any bleeding and bathe wounds with warm antiseptic water to remove any debris. As dogs' teeth carry bacteria, infection will invariably follow a bite wound. Abscesses may result, especially in deep puncture wounds. Antibiotic injections or tablets given at the time of the bite should prevent this. Larger wounds may need stitching and should be protected until examined by a vet.

FITS

There are a considerable number of reasons why dogs have a fit;

luckily Borders do not seem prone to them. I have seen puppies fit that have been totally infested with worms. Once de-wormed they never have another fit. A puppy may fit soon after the first primary vaccination, due to a reaction; this is rare, but the vet must be consulted, and should be able to correct this problem.

Any dog suffering a fit is quite frightening to observe. The signs are that the dog will collapse, possibly froth at the mouth, go rigid and the legs will start to move as if running, and there may be loss of control of bladder and bowels. While this is happening do not interfere, but ensure the dog can do no harm to himself while thrashing about. When the dog comes out of a fit he will be extremely weak and confused and will stand and walk as if drunk. Put the dog, at this point, in a safe, enclosed, darkened place where he will be quiet, until he has recovered. If the dog has another fit it would be sensible to take the dog to the vet. If epilepsy is diagnosed there are drugs that will control it.

HEATSTROKE

This is an acute emergency which happens during hot weather. It

can occur in dogs that have been shut in a car without sufficient ventilation. Remember that a car on a hot day creates a greenhouse effect and the temperature inside the car will increase rapidly. A dog can become severely distressed in minutes and die very, very quickly. Even with windows well open, a dog should never be shut in a car on a hot day. On cooler days the windows must be left open and grilles fitted.

A heatstroke victim will be severely distressed, frantically panting and will probably collapse. His temperature will be extremely high and, to bring it down, the dog's body should be submerged in cool water or hosed down with water. Do not use very cold water as this will cause more problems. When the temperature returns to normal the dog should be dried and put in a cool place to recover. The dog should have drinking water available at all stages, preferably with salt added (one dessertspoonful of salt per litre of water). If the dog does not recover quickly it would be advisable to take him to the vet as he may be suffering from shock. Border Terriers can be and have been victims of heatstroke; with their double coats they can feel the effects of heat quickly. The blue and tan colour of Borders appears to absorb the heat more easily, so extra care should be taken if your dog is this colour.

LAMENESS

Dogs will go lame for a multitude of reasons but the most common causes are found in the foot. If your dog is lame, check the pads for cuts, cracks, dried mud between the pads, thistles or any kind of swelling. Check the nails have not been damaged or that the nailbed is not infected. Sores between the pads can also cause lameness. If you find a foreign body in the foot, remove it and clean the foot with warm antiseptic water. An infected nailbed will need antibiotic treatment from the vet. This condition is very painful and should be treated quickly otherwise the nail will drop off,

which can cause further serious problems. A damaged nail, if down to the nailbed, should be bandaged to stop the dog knocking it further. Do be careful about bandaging feet as more serious harm can be caused if it is done incorrectly. Get professional help if in doubt.

If nothing appears wrong in the foot you must start to go up the leg, feeling for any swellings, lumps or cuts. Feel the opposite leg and compare the shape and size. Find out if there is any difference in the heat of the legs; bend the joints and move the leg. The dog may (or may not, in the case of Border Terriers being stoical when in pain) flinch when you touch the injury. Some dogs will be lame one day and, after resting overnight, will be completely sound the next. However, if your dog's lameness is still undetected and has not improved after two days, a vet's opinion should be sought.

PARASITES – EXTERNAL

Fleas are a common parasite and can act as an intermediate host for other dog parasites, but the main problem they cause is skin irritation. When a flea bites it injects saliva to stop the blood

clotting while it sucks it up. The saliva can cause an allergic reaction in the dog. The main sign that your dog has fleas is the black gritty substance found on the dog's coat. If you are not sure whether this is flea debris, collect some of the black grit from the coat and put on a wet, white tissue. If the black grit when wet goes blood-coloured, your dog has fleas. Treat the dog as quickly as possible, also his bedding and around the house. There are many excellent flea-control preparations on the market today, but I find that the veterinary-administered products are the most effective.

Ticks are found on dogs, usually through the summer months, and are parasites of sheep and cattle. The adult tick starts life small and spider-like. It crawls over the body, finds a suitable place and bites into the skin. It will stay in this position for about two weeks until fully engorged with blood, swollen to the size of a pea and beige in colour. The tick will then drop off the host and, if female, lay eggs in the grass. These hatch into larvae which will then find a host. After a feed, these larvae drop off, undergo change and find another host. It takes three larvae changes, each taking a year, before the adult form is arrived at and the cycle is then repeated. Ticks can be removed by using flea-control remedies, some of which are also designed to remove ticks. Other methods involve removing the tick by special forceps, making sure you grasp the head. This is made easier by killing the tick first. If you do not take the tick out complete with head you may end up with nastily infected skin.

Lice are grey, about 2mm long and they lay small eggs (nits) which stick to the dog's hair and can look like scurf. Dogs can scratch and create bald patches. Give repeat treatments of insecticide sprays or baths to kill the adults and any hatching larvae.

Harvest mites infestation occurs in the late summer, starting around late July. They are little orange mites which affect the feet, legs and skin of the belly and can cause immense irritation. The orange mite can just be seen with a naked eye. Treat with benzyl benzoate, a white emulsion which can be bought at the chemist, which should be rubbed into the affected parts. Many of the flea insecticides will also treat this complaint.

PARASITES – INTERNAL

Roundworms (Toxocara Canis) feed on digesting food in the dog's gut and are particularly harmful to puppies. They penetrate a puppy's gut wall and pass, by way of the blood, to the liver and then to the lungs. From there they crawl up the windpipe to be coughed up and swallowed, again ending up in the gut. Infected puppies may develop hepatitis, pneumonia, fits and obstruction in the gut. As the puppy gets older most of the worms travel to the muscles, where they form cysts. These lie dormant until the puppy (if a bitch) becomes pregnant, when they migrate to the embryo puppies' lungs; therefore every puppy is born with roundworm and must be wormed frequently.

Roundworm is the worm that can affect humans, causing blindness in a child. This happens extremely rarely but good hygiene and good sense concerning children and puppies should control the problem.

Tapeworms (Dipylidium caninum) are transmitted by fleas in which the larvae develop. Segments of the worm look like small grains of rice and can be seen in a dog's faeces. They can irritate the anus and cause discomfort. Modern tapeworm treatments are very effective and your vet will advise on how often you should treat your dog. It would be advisable to treat your dog and house for fleas at the same time.

PHANTOM PREGNANCY

Border bitches seem particularly prone to this condition. As bitches come in season on average every six months, starting as young as six to seven months, this problem can become a real inconvenience. At around six to seven weeks after the end of her season, about the time she would have had puppies had she been mated, the bitch will change her behaviour, going off her food, becoming quiet and then starting to dig in her bed or

making nests in odd places. She may start collecting toys and guarding them like newly-born puppies. The bitch can change character completely, becoming unreliable with the family, almost as if she has a mental disorder. Her mammary glands will fill with milk which can be a real nuisance to get rid of.

The whole condition can be treated by time and by effort from you. Keep the bitch busy, increase her exercise considerably, remove the toys, make her bed less cosy. Reduce her food slightly and restrict her drinking water to dry up the milk. If the milk refuses to go away, tablets from the vet will cure the problem. The bitch should return to normal after a couple of weeks. Phantom pregnancies can be avoided by having your bitch spayed.

PYOMETRA
This is an infection of the womb. It normally affects the bitch about six to eight weeks after being in season, but can occur at any time. The bitch will appear off-colour and develop an excessive thirst, vomiting and dullness, and the discharge from the vulva will be an abnormal colour, yellow, green or red and thick. If you think your bitch may have this condition it is essential to get her to the vet as quickly as possible. Life-saving surgery may be needed to remove the ovaries and womb. In mild cases drugs may settle the problem temporarily.

SHOCK
Shock is a complicated and serious clinical syndrome which leads to an inadequate blood supply to vital organs. If not attended to, death can and does occur. It is shock, not fractures, that is the major cause of death after road accidents and the likelihood of delayed shock is the reason why most vets will suggest a thorough examination and a short stay in the veterinary hospital for a road accident victim.

Shock is identified by unconsciousness, extreme weakness, the dog's skin feeling cold (especially ears), pale gums, a rapid heartbeat and rapid breathing. Shock is caused by massive decrease in blood, usually as a result of bleeding which, of course, may be internal. Large fluid losses caused by burns and scalds can cause shock. Severe stress or trauma, such as the extensive injuries and pain following a road accident, can also

lead to shock. Immediate veterinary attention is essential; this is a true emergency. Keep the dog warm while transporting him to the vet's surgery. If the dog is unconscious, lie him on his side and pull out the tongue to ensure the airway is clear. On arrival at the surgery the dog will quickly be put on an intravenous fluid drip.

SKIN PROBLEMS

Acute Moist Dermatitis (Wet Eczema) is a localised, wet, painful, acute inflammation of the skin which causes excessive scratching or licking by the dog. It often occurs on the rump and the initial irritation is thought to be impaction of the anal glands, although fleas are a possibility. The initial cause is not known but is thought to be a secondary reaction to flea bites. If not treated, the inflamed area can quickly become extensive.

Demodectic Mange is almost exclusively seen in puppies of three to nine months of age. The demodectic mite lives in the hair follicles and is thought to be present in most dogs in small numbers, causing no symptoms. In some puppies, for unknown reasons, the mite starts to multiply causing, at the beginning, bald patches to appear around the face and legs. Initially there is no irritation and so the puppy does not scratch. When the disease progresses the area of hair loss increases, the damaged skin becomes infected and the puppy may now start to scratch. Severely infected dogs will become depressed and bald. The skin becomes thick with black pigmentation and greasy with an unpleasant smell. Demodectic mites are passed from mother to puppy and, in most cases, never cause a problem. It is believed that the main cause for demodectic mange is stress-related. Veterinary attention is essential and the condition can be cleared up by intensive treatment.

Sarcoptic Mange is caused by a parasitic mite which lives in the skin and causes intense irritation. The most usualy affected areas are muzzle, ear flap, belly and legs. An affected dog will scratch constantly, which causes inflammation of the skin and hair loss. If the dog is not treated he will damage the skin and infect the skin with bacteria. In some cases the skin will become thickened, pigmented and scurfy. The dog will lose weight and be depressed. Veterinary treatment is essential and will be intensive. Sarcoptic mange is highly infectious among dogs and may mean you have to treat any other dogs you own or are in contact with. Housing and bedding should also be treated.

Cheyletiella Mange is caused by a microscopic mite which, on first appearance, looks like dandruff and usually appears on the back of the dog. Some dogs are extremely irritated by this mite and will roll about on the ground trying to relieve the aggravation. It is treated with a wash obtainable from the vet; again, it is contagious.

STINGS

Most dogs will snap at bees and wasps and Borders are no exception. The areas most likely to be stung are the mouth and tongue and, occasionally, the feet. If it is a bee sting and it is visible, try to pull it out; tweezers might be useful if the sting is in an awkward place. Bathe the sting area with bicarbonate of soda. If your dog is stung in the mouth then veterinary help should be called upon as the dog may be allergic to the sting and huge swellings will appear in the mouth and throat. An antihistamine injection will be essential.

SUMMARY

In this book I have tried to cover many of the questions I get asked regarding the Border Terrier, and to give the information sometimes required, over the years, while owning a Border.

The Border Terrier is basically an uncomplicated, robust, spirited little dog, renowned for adaptability and

an excellent temperament. Your Border should, given good fortune, enjoy a long, trouble-free, happy life.

Never be complacent about the care and attention you bestow on your Border. It is up to you to keep your dog healthy, happy and fit which, in turn, will bring you years of immense pleasure.